SUCCESSION PLANNING-

In Selecting a Leader of a Family Owned Business in Indian Context

This Book IS DEDICATED to my parents,
wife and children

ABOUT THE AUTHOR:

Mr Rajendra prasad Dhanuka is a Graduate in Electrical Engineering (1971). He served various big industries of India for more than 50 years.

Mr Dhanuka held senior positions in corporate world as senior President or as an advisor.

He had conducted various classes in general public as well as for the corporate world in India and abroad.

He has also got post Graduate Diploma in Counselling Psychology. He is certified practitioner of Neuro Linguistics Programming (NLP) and Mind Development for which he was trained by the inventors themselves.

Table of Contents

Chapter No.	Subjects	Page No.
1	Overview of succession planning	7
2	Importance of Succession Planning	11
3	Unique aspects of Indian family-owned businesses	13
4	Understanding family-owned businesses in India	16
5	Definition and characteristics of family owned businesses	18
6	Historical context of family owned businesses	20
7	Examples of family owned businesses	25
8	What is succession planning	28
9	Benefits of effective succession planning	29
10	Risk of inadequate succession planning	31
11	Key challenges in succession planning	36
12	Cultural Factors	38
13	Legal & regulatory considerations	40
14	Issues related to family dynamics & conflicts	42
15	Key factors in respect to economic & market pressures	44
16	Models of succession planning	47
17	Traditional Models of succession planning	49
18	Modern approaches to succession planning	50
19	Case studies of successful & unsuccessful succession planning	53
20	Developing a succession plan	56
21	Steps in creating a succession planning	58
22	Identifying & grooming potential successor	61
23	Training & Development for the successor	63
24	Structuring ownership and management transition	66

Chapter No.	Subjects	Page No.
25	Governance structure and succession planning	70
26	Role of family councils and Board of Directors	73
27	Implementing effective governance structures	75
28	Balancing interest with professional management	78
29	Legal and financial considerations	83
30	Legal framework for succession planning	86
31	Financial planning and asset management	88
32	Tax implications and estate planning	91
33	Detailed analysis of successful succession planning	94
34	Examination of challenges faced and lessons learned	98
35	Importance of involving external advisors	101
36	How to select and work with external advisors	102
37	Case studies of successful interventions	105
38	Emerging trend in succession planning	109
39	Impact of Technology & globalisation	111
40	Preparing for future challenges	113
41	Summary of Key Points	117
42	Final Thoughts	119
43	Recommendations for successful planning	120
44	Samples of succession planning	123
45	List of Useful resources & readings	127
46	Glossary if Terms	129
47	Comprehensive list of sources	132

PREFACE

In the vibrant landscape of Indian family-owned businesses, the intertwining of tradition and modernity presents both unique challenges and unparalleled opportunities. As these enterprises have thrived over generations, the question of succession planning emerges as a crucial element for ensuring their longevity and continued success. This book is a culmination of my insights, research, and a collaborative journey that have enriched my understanding of this vital topic.

Drawing on the experiences of family-owned enterprises across India, I have sought to weave together a wealth of information, distil best practices, and present actionable strategies tailored to the distinct cultural and economic fabric of our country. As you navigate through these pages, you will encounter stories of resilience, lessons from failures, and frameworks designed to facilitate meaningful conversations about the future. Whether you are a current leader, a prospective successor, or an advisor, I hope this book serves as a valuable resource to inspire thoughtful succession planning that honours the past while embracing the future.

In a rapidly evolving business environment, the ability to adapt and prepare for change is essential. I invite you to embark on this journey, not only to safeguard the legacy of your family business but also to empower the next generation to lead with confidence and vision.

Succession Planning used to be given full importance even in our ancient times for smooth transfer of legacy, administration, governance and ultimately the kingdom to the next generation. If they did not find a proper candidate in the family, they did not hesitate to select a suitable candidate from outside.

contd..

There was a King Bharat who was the son of King Dushyanta and Queen Shakuntala who was the daughter of Rishi Vishwamitra. King Bharat was a very powerful and courageous King, unique in governance and administration.

He spread his kingdom from the Himalayas in the north to the Seas in the south almost resembling the map of India today. There are so many leaders named Bharat in our ancient history. Here I am mentioning the Bharat who was the ancestor of all.

Kauravas and Pandavas. Bharat could not find any of his sons (he was having 9 sons) suitable as his successor so a saint's son Bhardwaj Bhimanyu was chosen as the successor of Bharat (Mahabharata).

Bharat chose the name of his kingdom 'Bharatvarsha' that time and today also we call this country "Bharat". He could rule the country very successfully. He would not compromise in selecting his successor, so he did not choose any of his own sons as his successor. Rather he selected Bhimanyu as his successor who later became the ancestor of the powerful Kauravas and Pandavas and ruled Hastinapur very successfully.

Succession planning is not merely a logistical necessity; it is an intricate process that demands emotional intelligence, strategic foresight, and an appreciation for the family's legacy. While many businesses focus on financial growth and operational efficiency, the transition of leadership often remains an overlooked aspect, leading to potential disruptions and conflicts. This book aims to bridge that gap.

Rajendra Prasad Dhanuka

GROUP: I

INTRODUCTION

Subject	Chapter No.
Overview of Succession Planning	1
Importance of Succession Planning for family-owned businesses	2
Unique aspects of Indian family-owned businesses	3

Succession Planning is not an event; it is a process. And it's never too early to start – Warren Buffet.

CHAPTER 1

CHAPTER: 1

Overview of succession planning in family-owned big businesses in Indian context

Succession planning in family-owned big businesses in India is a critical yet complex process, influenced by cultural, legal, and economic factors. Here's an overview of the key aspects:

Cultural Factors: Indian family businesses often have strong familial ties, which influence succession planning. Traditionally, the eldest son or a family member is expected to take over leadership roles. However, this is evolving, with more families recognizing the need for merit-based succession.

Leadership Transition: Effective succession planning involves preparing the next generation for leadership roles through formal education and practical experience. Family businesses often face challenges in balancing family expectations with professional competencies.

Governance Structures: Many large family-owned businesses are establishing formal governance structures, such as family councils and advisory boards, to support succession planning. These structures help in setting clear guidelines for leadership transition and resolving family conflicts.

Legal and Financial Planning: Succession planning includes legal and financial considerations, such as estate planning, tax implications, and restructuring of ownership. Legal frameworks, including wills and trusts, are used to manage inheritance and avoid disputes.

Professionalization: There is a growing trend towards professionalizing management by hiring non-family executives. This helps in bringing in external perspectives and skills while ensuring that family members are groomed to take on strategic roles.

Challenges: Common challenges include resistance to change, generational conflicts, and the need for balancing family interests with business needs. Ensuring smooth communication and planning for potential conflicts are crucial

Succession planning in respect to family-owned businesses in Indian context can be particularly challenging, and there have been several notable cases. Here are a few examples of succession planning cases which are flourishing and growing and/or some of them are examples of having set back due to lack of proper succession planning.

Example 1: The families which are flourishing and growing with proper succession planning.

1. **Tata Group:** The Tata Group has a long history of effective succession planning, with the transition from Jamshedji Tata to Ratan Tata and now to Natarajan Chandrasekaran as chairman. The group emphasizes professional management alongside family involvement, ensuring continuity and growth.

2. **Wadia Group:** The Wadia Group has navigated generational transitions effectively. The family has embraced professional management, allowing younger family members to take on leadership roles while still being guided by seasoned professionals.

3. Godrej Group: The Godrej family has implemented a structured succession plan that includes training and development for younger family members. This has facilitated smooth transitions and the ability to adapt to market changes, contributing to the group's ongoing success.

4. Mahindra Group: The Mahindra Group has established a robust governance framework, which includes clear succession planning processes. Anand Mahindra's leadership has successfully integrated family values with professional management, leading to growth and innovation.

5. Reliance Industries: Mukesh Ambani's management of Reliance has included a clear vision for succession planning, especially regarding his children. By involving them in various aspects of the business early on, he ensures preparedness for future leadership roles.

6. Hindustan Unilever: Although a subsidiary of Unilever, the Indian arm has seen effective succession planning through the involvement of family members in leadership roles and by fostering a culture of professional development.

These businesses exemplify the importance of integrating professional management, strategic planning, and family values to ensure long-term success.

Example 2: The families which were having setbacks without proper succession planning.

1. The Goenka Family (RPG Enterprises): After the death of Dr. Harsh Goenka's father, there was significant conflict over leadership roles among family members. The lack of a clear succession plan led to disputes that affected the company's performance and strategic direction.

2. The Mallya Family (Kingfisher Airlines): Vijay Mallya's failure to effectively transition leadership and management roles to his children resulted in a series of mismanagement issues. The lack of a structured plan contributed to the airline's eventual collapse.

3. The Kirloskar Family: Disputes among family members over control of the Kirloskar Group led to a split. The absence of a formal succession strategy resulted in a prolonged legal battle and fragmentation of the business.

4. The Tatas: While Tata Group is often seen as a successful family business, the transition of leadership between Ratan Tata and his successor was fraught with challenges. The decision-making process revealed underlying family tensions that could have been mitigated with better planning.

5. The Birla Family: The split of the Aditya Birla Group into multiple entities after the death of Aditya Vikram Birla highlighted the consequences of inadequate succession planning. Family conflicts over leadership and direction have led to fragmentation and operational inefficiencies.

These cases illustrate the critical need for clear succession planning, open communication, and conflict resolution mechanisms in family-owned businesses. Overall, succession planning in Indian family-owned big businesses requires a strategic approach to manage the unique blend of family dynamics and business goals.

CHAPTER: 2

Importance of succession planning for family-owned businesses in India

Succession planning is crucial for family-owned businesses in India for several reasons:

1. Continuity: It ensures the business continues operating smoothly after the current leaders retire or pass away, reducing the risk of disruption.

2. Preservation of Legacy: It helps preserve the family's legacy and values, maintaining the company's ethos and culture through generations.

3. Conflict Reduction: Proper planning can mitigate family disputes and conflicts over leadership and ownership, providing a clear path for transition.

4. Talent Development: It provides an opportunity to identify and groom potential leaders within the family, ensuring they are prepared to take on responsibilities.

5. Financial Stability: A well-structured succession plan can enhance the financial stability of the business, making it more attractive to investors and creditors.

6. Business Growth: With a clear plan in place, the business can focus on growth and strategic initiatives, rather than dealing with uncertainty and leadership crises.

In the context of India, where many businesses are family-owned and deeply tied to cultural values, effective succession planning is key to ensuring long-term success and stability.

7. Long-Term Sustainability: Family businesses in India often have a long history and a deep connection to their founding families. Effective succession planning ensures that the business can continue to thrive and maintain its legacy across generations.

8. Family Dynamics: Indian family businesses frequently involve complex family dynamics, which can impact decision-making and governance. Succession planning helps address potential conflicts and clarifies roles, reducing the risk of disputes that can arise when leadership transitions are not well-managed.

9. Cultural and Social Expectations: In Indian culture, there is a strong emphasis on family ties and maintaining the family's honour and reputation. Succession planning aligns with these cultural expectations by preparing the next generation to take on leadership roles responsibly.

10. Economic Impact: Family-owned businesses contribute significantly to the Indian economy. Ensuring that these businesses are well-prepared for leadership transitions helps preserve jobs and economic stability within communities.

11. Legal and Financial Complexity: Indian family businesses often face legal and financial complexities, including issues related to inheritance laws and taxation. Succession planning helps navigate these complexities and ensures that the transition is legally and financially sound.

12. Professionalization: As businesses grow, there's often a need to professionalize operations and governance. Succession planning facilitates this process by preparing the next generation to manage and lead the business in a more structured and professional manner.

In summary, for family-owned businesses in India, succession planning is crucial for maintaining family harmony, ensuring business continuity, and navigating legal and cultural complexities

CHAPTER 3

Unique aspects of Indian family-owned businesses.

Indian family-owned businesses often have several unique aspects:

1. Long-Term Vision: Many are driven by a long-term vision, focusing on sustaining the business across generations rather than short-term profits.

2. Strong Family Ties: The family often plays a central role in decision-making, which can lead to a cohesive company culture but may also result in conflicts if family dynamics are strained.

3. Flexibility and Adaptability: These businesses tend to be more flexible and adaptable, leveraging personal relationships and informal networks to navigate challenges.

4. Emphasis on Relationships: There is a strong emphasis on maintaining relationships with customers, suppliers, and other stakeholders, often leading to high levels of trust and loyalty.

5. Traditional Practices: Many family-owned businesses adhere to traditional business practices and values, which can impact their approach to innovation and modernization.

6. Generational Transfer: Succession planning is a critical issue, with a focus on transferring leadership to the next generation while managing the potential for conflicts and ensuring continuity.

7. Social Responsibility: There is often a strong sense of social responsibility and community involvement, reflecting traditional values and a commitment to giving back to society.

8. Hierarchical Structure: The organizational structure can be more hierarchical, with significant influence held by senior family members, which may affect decision-making processes and governance.

These aspects contribute to the unique character and operational dynamics of Indian family-owned businesses.

GROUP II

Subject	Chapter No.
Understanding family-owned businesses in India	4
Definition of Characteristics of family-owned businesses.	5
Historical Context and Evolution of Family businesses in India	6
Examples of Prominent family-owned businesses.	7

The future of any Organization depends on its ability to develop and maintain a steady stream of capable leaders – Jack Welch.

CHAPTER 4

Understanding family-owned businesses in India.

Family-owned businesses are a significant part of India's economic landscape. They often encompass a wide range of industries, from manufacturing and retail to services and technology. Here are some key aspects to understand about them:

1. Historical Context: Many of India's family-owned businesses have deep historical roots, often starting as small enterprises and growing into large conglomerates over generations.

2. Governance: Governance structures in family-owned businesses can vary. Some have formal boards and professional managers, while others rely on family members for decision-making. The degree of professionalism often influences their growth and adaptability.

3. Succession Planning: Succession planning is a crucial issue. Many businesses face challenges in transitioning leadership from one generation to the next, balancing familial relationships with professional management.

4. Cultural Influence: Family values and cultural traditions often play a significant role in how these businesses operate. This can affect everything from management styles to business strategies.

5. Economic Impact: These businesses contribute significantly to employment and economic development in India. They often have a strong presence in local and regional markets.

6. Challenges: Common challenges include managing family dynamics, maintaining business growth, and adapting to changing market conditions. Additionally, they may face issues with formalizing processes and governance structures.

Understanding these aspects can provide insight into how family-owned businesses operate and their impact on the Indian economy.

CHAPTER 5

Definition and characteristics of family-owned businesses

A family-owned business is a commercial enterprise where a majority of the ownership and control lies within a single family. Here are some key characteristics:

1. Ownership: The family holds significant ownership stakes, often controlling a substantial portion of the shares or equity in the company.

2. Control: Family members are typically involved in the management and decision-making processes, exerting significant influence over the company's operations and strategic direction.

3. Succession Planning: Family-owned businesses often have plans for passing leadership and ownership from one generation to the next, which can affect long-term strategy and stability.

4. Values and Culture: These businesses often reflect the values, traditions, and culture of the family, which can influence company policies and practices.

5. Long-term Focus: Family businesses may prioritize long-term stability and growth over short-term profits, driven by the desire to build a lasting legacy.

6. Decision-Making: Decisions may be influenced by family dynamics and relationships, which can impact the company's operations and management style.

7. Resource Allocation: Family-owned businesses might have more flexibility in resource allocation, including investment decisions, based on family interests and long-term goals.

These characteristics can create unique advantages, such as strong commitment and loyalty, but also pose challenges like potential conflicts and succession issues.

CHAPTER 6

Historical Context of Family-Owned Businesses in India

Ancient and Medieval Periods

Family-owned businesses in India have deep historical roots, dating back to ancient and medieval periods. Trade guilds, known as SHRENIS, were formed in ancient India, facilitating commerce and promoting collective interests among traders. These guilds often operated as family-run enterprises, passing knowledge and wealth through generations.

Examples from ancient, premediaeval period or from recent past regarding wise and most astute decision for India in succession planning. India's history offers several examples of wise decision-making in succession planning, particularly during critical transitions of power:

1. Maurya Empire (Chandragupta Maurya): Chandragupta's strategic decision to ensure the succession of his son, Bindusara, was crucial for maintaining the stability of the empire. His choice of a capable successor helped preserve the unity and strength of the Mauryan dynasty.

2. Gupta Empire (Chandragupta I to Samudragupta): The transition from Chandragupta I to his son Samudragupta exemplifies effective succession planning. Samudragupta's military and administrative skills allowed for the expansion and consolidation of the Gupta Empire, ensuring its legacy.

3. Mughal Empire (Akbar to Jahangir): Akbar's decision to groom his son Jahangir for leadership, alongside establishing a council of advisors, facilitated a smooth transition. This planning helped sustain the empire's cultural and political achievements.

4. Maratha Empire (Shivaji to Shambhaji): Shivaji's focus on ensuring a clear line of succession for his son Shambhaji, despite challenges, emphasized the importance of preparation and training in leadership roles, which was essential for the Maratha's resilience.

5. Indian National Congress (Gandhi to Nehru): Mahatma Gandhi's mentoring of Jawaharlal Nehru highlighted the importance of succession in the Indian independence movement. Nehru's leadership helped shape modern India post-independence, showing how strategic succession can influence a nation's future.

These examples illustrate the significance of careful planning and mentorship in leadership transitions throughout India's history.

Colonial Era: During British colonial rule, many Indian businesses flourished despite economic constraints. Prominent families like the TATAS and BIRLAS emerged, leveraging trade opportunities and establishing industries such as textiles, steel, and banking. This era saw the formalization of family businesses, with an emphasis on familial loyalty and succession.

Post-Independence Era: After India gained independence in 1947, the government implemented various economic policies that favoured large-scale industries, often led by family-owned businesses. The License Raj restricted entrepreneurship, but families like the Tatas, Birla's, and Mahindra's adapted by diversifying their portfolios, investing in infrastructure and manufacturing.

Evolution of Family-Owned Businesses Liberalization in 1990s:
The economic liberalization of the 1990s transformed the landscape for family businesses. With reduced regulations, many family firms expanded into new sectors and embraced modern management practices. Globalization opened new markets, leading to increased competition but also new opportunities for growth.

Current Landscape: Today, family-owned businesses contribute significantly to India's economy. They account for a substantial portion of GDP, employment, and exports. Many have transitioned into professional management structures while still retaining family control. However, the balance between family influence and professional governance is often delicate.

Succession Planning Challenges:

1. Cultural Factors:

In Indian society, familial ties are paramount, influencing decision-making and succession. There's often a reluctance to transfer control to non-family members, even when it might benefit the business.

2. Generational Differences:

Younger generations may have different visions and values, often seeking modernization and innovation. Tensions between traditional practices and modern business strategies can complicate succession.

3. Conflict Resolution:

Family dynamics can lead to conflicts over leadership roles, decision-making authority, and inheritance, impacting business continuity.

4. Legal and Tax Considerations:

Estate planning and tax implications play a crucial role in succession planning. Families must navigate Indian laws concerning inheritance, taxation, and business ownership.

5. Professionalization:

Many family businesses struggle with the transition to a professional management model, which is essential for long-term sustainability. This requires clear governance structures and strategic planning.

Best Practices in Succession Planning

1. Early Planning:

Families should begin succession planning well in advance, involving all stakeholders to create a transparent process.

2. Formal Governance Structures:

Establishing a board of directors or advisory board can help in making objective decisions and reducing familial tensions.

3. Education and Training:

Preparing the next generation through mentorship and formal education in business management can equip them for leadership roles.

4. Open Communication:

Fostering a culture of open dialogue about business goals and family expectations can help mitigate conflicts.

5. Legal Framework:

Engaging legal and financial advisors to create a robust estate plan can safeguard against disputes and ensure smooth transitions.

The evolution of family-owned businesses in India is a testament to their resilience and adaptability. As these enterprises navigate the complexities of succession planning, balancing tradition with modernity will be key to their sustainability and growth in the future. By embracing best practices and addressing inherent challenges, family businesses can ensure their legacy continues to thrive.

CHAPTER: 7

Examples of prominent family-owned businesses (like-Tata, Birla, Reliance, Mahindra to name a few) to understand their succession planning in businesses

Here are some prominent family-owned businesses and insights into their succession planning

1. Tata Group: Founded by Jamshedji Tata, the group emphasizes a strong governance structure. Succession planning is often based on merit, with family members being groomed for leadership roles through various group companies.

2. Birla Group: The Birla family has a history of strong succession planning, often involving professional management alongside family members. The focus is on maintaining the family's vision while adapting to market changes.

3. Reliance Industries: Founded by Dhirubhai Ambani, succession planning became critical after his passing. The company is now managed by his sons, Mukesh and Anil, with clear roles defined and a focus on professionalization to ensure stability.

4. Mahindra Group: The Mahindra family employs a structured approach to succession planning, promoting family members with relevant experience. They also engage in leadership development programs for future leaders.

5. Wipro: Founded by the Premji family, Wipro has seen a shift to professional management. The family's involvement is strategic, with clear succession plans that allow for both family and non-family executives to lead.

6. Godrej Group: The Godrej family practices a blend of family leadership and professional management. They emphasize grooming future leaders through hands-on experience and mentorship.

7. Aditya Birla Group: This group has a clear succession plan that integrates both family involvement and professional management. The emphasis is on maintaining the entrepreneurial spirit while ensuring stability.

8. Cargill: Although not solely family-owned, the Cargill family plays a significant role in management. They focus on grooming future generations through education and hands-on experience in various business areas.

Key Aspects of Their Succession Planning:

Merit-Based Leadership: Many of these businesses prioritize merit and experience in succession decisions, ensuring capable leadership.

Professional Management: A shift towards professional management alongside family members is common, balancing family values with business acumen.

Long-Term Vision: Succession planning often aligns with a long-term vision, ensuring that future leaders uphold the company's core values and culture.

Mentorship and Training: Family members are frequently mentored and trained within the business to prepare them for leadership roles.

Group: III

Subject	Chapter No.
What is succession Planning ?	8
Benefits of effective succession planning.	9
Risks of inadequate succession planning.	10

A great person attracts great people and knows how to hold them together- Johann Wolfgang Von Gothe.

CHAPTER: 8

What is succession planning particularly in family-owned businesses in India

Succession planning in family-owned businesses in India involves developing strategies to ensure a smooth transition of leadership and ownership from one generation to the next. This process is crucial for maintaining stability, preserving family legacy, and ensuring business continuity.

Key aspects include:

1. Identifying Successors: Determining who will take over leadership roles, often involving family members who have shown interest and capability.

2. Training and Development: Providing the necessary education and experience to prepare successors for their future roles.

3. Communication: Open discussions among family members about roles, expectations, and potential conflicts are essential to foster understanding and alignment.

4. Legal and Financial Considerations: Addressing ownership structures, wills, and taxation issues to avoid disputes and ensure fair distribution.

5. Cultural Factors: In India, cultural values such as respect for elders and family unity play a significant role in shaping succession decisions.

6. External Advisors: Many families engage consultants or advisors to facilitate the planning process, offering unbiased perspectives.

CHAPTER: 9

Benefits of effective succession planning for family businesses particularly in Indian contexts. Here are some key benefits

1. Continuity and Stability: Succession planning ensures a smooth transition of leadership, maintaining business continuity and stability during changes.

2. Preservation of Family Legacy: It helps in preserving the family's values and legacy, reinforcing the identity and mission of the business.

3. Conflict Minimization: By establishing clear roles and responsibilities, succession planning reduces potential conflicts among family members regarding leadership and ownership.

4. Skill Development: It encourages the development of future leaders within the family, ensuring they are well-prepared to take on management roles.

5. Financial Security: Effective planning can lead to better financial management, as it often includes strategies for tax efficiency and wealth distribution among family members.

6. Enhanced Reputation: A well-executed succession plan can enhance the business's reputation, demonstrating professionalism and stability to customers, suppliers, and investors.

7. Adaptability to Change: It allows the business to adapt more readily to market changes, as successors can bring new perspectives and innovations.

8. Legal and Regulatory Compliance: Succession planning helps in navigating legal and regulatory requirements, reducing risks associated with ownership transfer.

9. Emotional Preparedness: It prepares family members emotionally for transitions, reducing stress and uncertainty during leadership changes.

10. Long-term Growth: With a clear vision for the future, businesses can better strategize for long-term growth, ensuring sustainability across generations.
In the Indian context, these benefits are amplified by the importance of familial ties, cultural values, and the unique challenges posed by a rapidly changing business environment.

CHAPTER: 10

Risks of inadequate succession planning for family-owned businesses in Indian contexts

Inadequate succession planning in family-owned businesses in India can lead to several significant risks, which can threaten the stability and longevity of the business. Here are some key risks in detail:

1. Leadership Vacuum:

• **Loss of Direction**: Without a clear successor, the business may struggle with decision-making, leading to a lack of strategic direction.

• **Operational Disruptions**: An abrupt leadership change can disrupt daily operations, affecting productivity and employee morale.

2. Family Conflicts:

• **Disputes Among Heirs**: In the absence of a clear succession plan, disagreements among family members over leadership roles or business direction can escalate, causing rifts and impacting business decisions.

• **Emotional Strain**: Personal relationships may suffer, which can further complicate business operations and decision-making processes.

3. Decreased Business Value:

- **Loss of Investor Confidence**: Uncertainty regarding leadership can deter investors, partners, and stakeholders, resulting in decreased financial support and market value.

- **Diminished Brand Reputation**: A lack of continuity may damage the brand's reputation, particularly if the transition appears chaotic or unprofessional.

4. Skill Gaps:

- **Inadequate Training**: If successors are not adequately prepared or trained, they may lack the necessary skills and knowledge to effectively manage the business.

- **Resistance to Change**: Successors may struggle to implement new ideas or adapt to market changes if they lack exposure and experience.

5. Financial Instability:

- **Loss of Revenue**: Operational disruptions and a decline in investor confidence can lead to decreased sales and revenue, affecting overall business sustainability.

- **Increased Costs**: Legal disputes or the need for external leadership can incur additional costs, straining financial resources.

6. Regulatory and Compliance Risks:

- **Legal Issues**: Failure to properly transition ownership can lead to legal disputes or non-compliance with regulations, especially in family businesses that are often complex in their structure.

• **Tax Implications**: Poor succession planning can result in unexpected tax liabilities that may strain financial resources and complicate business operations.

7. Loss of Institutional Knowledge:

• **Knowledge Gaps**: Key insights and experiences held by founding members may be lost if there's no structured transfer of knowledge to successors.

• **Declining Innovation**: Without effective knowledge transfer, the business may struggle to innovate, falling behind competitors.

8. Impact on Employees:

• **Decreased Morale**: Uncertainty about the future leadership can lead to low employee morale, increased turnover, and difficulty in attracting top talent.

• **Lack of Loyalty**: Employees may feel insecure about their jobs and future with the company, impacting their commitment and productivity.

9. Market Competitiveness:

• **Strategic Misalignment**: A lack of clear vision can result in strategic misalignments, making it difficult for the business to compete effectively in the market.

• **Slow Response to Market Changes**: Ineffective leadership transitions may lead to delays in responding to market demands or shifts, resulting in lost opportunities.

10. Long-term Sustainability:

• **Business Continuity Risks**: A lack of succession planning can jeopardize the long-term sustainability of the business, leading to its eventual decline or closure.

• **Legacy Concerns**: Founders may worry about their legacy and the ability of their successors to uphold the family values and vision.

Group: IV

Subject	Chapter No.
Key Challenges in succession planning for Indian family-owned businesses.	11
Cultural Factors influencing succession e.g. Traditional Values, Familial Obligations.	12
Legal and Regulatory considerations in India	13
Issues related to family dynamics and conflicts	14
Key factors in respect to Economic and Market pressures.	15

A leader is best when people barely know he exists- Lao Tzu

CHAPTER: 11

Key challenges in succession planning:

1. Family Dynamics: Conflicts among family members can complicate decision-making. Rivalries and differing visions for the future can hinder effective planning.

2. Lack of Formal Structures: Many family businesses operate informally, which can lead to unclear roles and responsibilities, making succession difficult.

3. Skill Gaps: Younger family members may lack the necessary skills or experience to take over leadership roles, especially in rapidly changing industries.

4. Resistance to Change: Established leaders may be reluctant to step back or adapt to new business practices, creating tension in the transition.

5. Cultural Factors: Cultural expectations and traditions can influence succession choices, sometimes favouring lineage over merit.

6. Regulatory and Legal Challenges: Navigating inheritance laws and tax implications can complicate the transfer of ownership and control.

7. Emotional Attachments: Strong emotional ties to the business can cloud judgement, making it hard to make objective decisions regarding leadership and direction.

8. Long-term vs. Short-term Goals: Balancing the immediate financial needs of the business with long-term strategic planning can be challenging.

9. External Competition: Rapidly changing market dynamics and competition may pressure family businesses, complicating succession planning.

10. Limited Awareness: Many families may not prioritize succession planning or lack awareness of its importance, leading to unpreparedness.

Addressing these challenges requires a combination of open communication, formal planning, and possibly external advisory support.

CHAPTER: 12

CULTURAL FACTORS:

Cultural factor becomes one of the key challenging points in influencing succession planning like as Traditional Values, Familial Obligations etc and those factors significantly impact succession planning, often creating challenges in organizations, especially family-owned businesses. Here are some key points to consider:

1. Traditional Values: In many cultures, respect for hierarchy and seniority can dictate succession choices, favouring older or more established family members over potentially more capable successors.

2. Familial Obligations: Family ties often prioritize keeping leadership within the family, even if external candidates may bring more expertise. This can lead to conflicts between merit-based and familial considerations.

3. Collectivism vs. Individualism: In collectivist cultures, group harmony and family loyalty can supersede individual ambition, potentially stifling the emergence of new leaders who may challenge the status quo.

4. Perceptions of Leadership: Cultural perceptions of leadership can influence who is considered a suitable successor. In some cultures, leadership traits may be associated with specific genders or family roles, limiting options.

5. Resistance to Change: Cultural inertia can create resistance to innovative succession strategies, making it difficult to implement new practices that might benefit the organization.

6. Communication Styles: Varied communication norms can complicate discussions about succession planning, leading to misunderstandings and a lack of clarity about expectations and goals.

CHAPTER: 13

Legal and regulatory consideration may be a challenging key factor that can complicate the process. Here are some key factors:

1. Inheritance Laws: Indian succession laws differ based on religion (Hindu, Muslim, Christian, etc.), affecting how assets are distributed among heirs. Understanding these laws is crucial to ensure compliance and avoid disputes.

2. Business Structure: The legal structure of the business (partnership, private limited company, etc.) impacts succession planning. Transitioning ownership may require restructuring to align with regulatory requirements.

3. Tax Implications: Succession can trigger various taxes, such as inheritance tax or capital gains tax. Careful tax planning is essential to minimize liabilities for both the business and the successors.

4. Corporate Governance: Compliance with the Companies Act and adherence to good governance practices are vital. This includes maintaining proper records, holding regular meetings, and ensuring transparency.

5. Dispute Resolution: Family businesses often face internal conflicts during succession. Establishing a clear dispute resolution mechanism, whether through mediation or arbitration, can help prevent legal battles.

6. Regulatory Approvals: Depending on the industry, transferring ownership may require approvals from regulatory bodies. Understanding these requirements is essential to avoid disruptions.

7. Employment Laws: Transitioning leadership may affect employee contracts and rights. Ensuring compliance with labour laws is critical to maintain workforce stability.

8. Family Agreements: Formalizing family agreements regarding succession can prevent misunderstandings and conflicts. These agreements should comply with legal standards to be enforceable.

CHAPTER: 14

Issues related to family dynamics and conflict for an Indian family-owned business at the time of succession planning:

Succession planning in an Indian family-owned business often involves complex family dynamics and conflicts. One challenging issue is the struggle between tradition and modernization. Elders may prefer to maintain established practices and keep leadership within the family, while younger members might advocate for professional management or diversification to adapt to changing market conditions.

This conflict can lead to:

1. Resistance to Change: Older generations might resist new ideas, fearing loss of control or the dilution of family values, causing friction with younger members seeking innovation.

2. Sibling Rivalry: In cases where multiple siblings are involved, differing visions for the future can create rivalries. Disputes over who should lead or how to split responsibilities can escalate into deeper conflicts.

3. Communication Barriers: Different communication styles across generations may result in misunderstandings, where younger members feel unheard and older members feel disrespected.

4. Equity vs. Equality: Deciding whether to distribute ownership equally among heirs or based on involvement can lead to feelings of favouritism or resentment, complicating family relationships.

5. Role Confusion: As roles shift during succession, conflicts can arise over authority, decision-making processes, and expectations, leading to power struggles.

Addressing these challenges requires open dialogue, clear communication, and sometimes the involvement of external mediators or advisors to facilitate a smoother transition.

CHAPTER: 15

Key factors in respect to Economic and Market pressures-

Succession planning in family-owned businesses faces several challenging key factors, particularly *under economic and market pressures*:

1. Emotional Dynamics: Family relationships can complicate decision-making. Emotional ties may hinder objective assessments of the next generation's capabilities and readiness.

2. Resistance to Change: Long-standing traditions and practices may resist new strategies or leadership styles, limiting adaptability in response to market changes.

3. Market Volatility: Economic downturns can strain resources, making it difficult to invest in succession planning or training future leaders.

4. Talent Shortages: Identifying and nurturing suitable successors within the family can be challenging, especially if there's a lack of interest or qualifications among heirs.

5. Strategic Vision: Aligning the family's vision with market realities requires balancing long-term goals with immediate financial pressures, often leading to conflicting priorities.

6. Financial Considerations: Valuation of the business and transfer of ownership can be complicated by fluctuating market conditions, affecting funding for transitions.

7. Regulatory Environment: Changes in laws and regulations can create uncertainty and impact succession strategies, particularly in terms of tax implications.

8. Stakeholder Expectations: Family businesses often juggle expectations from various stakeholders, including employees, customers, and community members, complicating succession plans.

9. Cultural Factors: Different cultural attitudes towards leadership and family roles can influence succession planning, making it crucial to understand and navigate these dynamics.

Group: V

Subject	Chapter No.
Models of Succession Planning Traditional	16
Models of succession in Indian family business	17
Modern approaches to succession planning	18
Case studies of successful and unsuccessful succession planning	19

The pessimist complains about the wind. The optimist expects to change. The leader adjusts sails – John Maxwell.

CHAPTER: 16

Models of succession planning in family-owned businesses in Indian context.

Succession planning in family-owned businesses in India is critical due to the unique cultural, social, and economic dynamics at play. Here are some prominent models and considerations relevant to the Indian context:

1. Traditional Succession Model

Family Hierarchy: Succession typically follows the family line, often favouring the eldest son or a chosen family member.

Role of Elders: Older family members often guide the process, ensuring the next generation understands the business ethos and values.

2. Professionalization Model

Incorporating Professionals: As businesses grow, families may bring in non-family executives to prepare the next generation for leadership.

Training and Development: Focus on education and professional training for successors to ensure they have the necessary skills.

3. Participatory Model

Involvement of Successors: Potential successors are involved in decision-making from an early age to build experience and confidence.

Mentorship Programs: Established family members mentor successors, promoting a culture of learning.

4. Hybrid Model

Combination of Family and Non-family: This approach blends family members and professional managers in leadership roles.

Flexibility: Allows for a more dynamic leadership structure that adapts to business needs.

5. Cultural and Emotional Considerations

Emotional Bonds: The close-knit nature of families in India can complicate succession due to emotional ties and conflicts.

Cultural Values: Respect for tradition and family legacy often influences decision-making.

6. Legal and Financial Planning

Estate Planning: Important to have clear legal frameworks to avoid disputes over inheritance and control.

Shareholder Agreements: Establishing clear guidelines can help manage expectations and responsibilities.

7. Case Studies and Best Practices

Successful Indian Families: Examining examples like the Tata Group or the Birla family can provide insights into effective succession strategies.

Adaptation and Resilience: Families that adapt their strategies to changing market conditions tend to succeed in the long term.

CHAPTER: 17

Traditional models of succession planning

Traditional models of succession in Indian family businesses often follow a few key patterns:

1. Primogeniture: The eldest son typically inherits the family business. This model is rooted in the belief that the firstborn has the most experience and is best positioned to lead.

2. Merit-based selection: Some families may choose a successor based on merit rather than birth order. This approach evaluates the capabilities and skills of all potential heirs, including daughters, which is becoming more common.

3. Family consensus: In some cases, the decision is made collectively by family members, focusing on harmony and agreement rather than a strict line of succession.

4. Professional management: Increasingly, families are appointing non-family professionals to manage the business, especially when the next generation lacks interest or expertise. This can lead to a hybrid model where family members retain ownership while professionals run the operations.

5. Phased succession: Some businesses implement a gradual transition, where the current leader mentors the successor over time. This allows for a smoother transfer of knowledge and leadership.

6. Involvement of women: Traditionally, women had limited roles in family businesses, but there is a growing trend of including daughters and female relatives in succession planning.

CHAPTER: 18

Modern approaches to succession planning in Indian family-owned businesses

Succession planning in Indian family-owned businesses has evolved significantly in recent years, reflecting modern approaches that blend tradition with contemporary practices. Here are some key trends:

1. Formalization of Processes

Structured Succession Plans: Many businesses are adopting formal succession planning frameworks that outline clear roles, responsibilities, and timelines for transition.

Documentation and Transparency: Increasing emphasis on documenting the succession process to ensure clarity and reduce ambiguity.

2. Professionalization

Involvement of Non-Family Professionals: Hiring external consultants and professionals to provide objective insights and facilitate smoother transitions.

Training and Development: Investing in the development of next-generation leaders through mentorship, training programs, and exposure to various business functions.

3. Strategic Governance Structures

Family Governance Policies: Establishing family councils and governance structures to address conflicts and align family members on business objectives.

Advisory Boards: Forming advisory boards that include non-family members to bring diverse perspectives and expertise.

4. Focus on Next-Gen Engagement

- **Involvement in Business Operations**: Encouraging younger family members to take active roles in the business early on to build experience and commitment.

- **Creating Opportunities for Leadership Roles**: Providing them with opportunities to lead specific projects or departments.

5. Emphasis on Values and Legacy

- **Preserving Family Values**: Integrating family values and legacy into the business strategy to maintain a sense of identity and continuity.

- **Philanthropic Engagement**: Involving the next generation in philanthropic activities to instil a sense of responsibility and connection to broader societal goals.

6. Use of Technology

- **Digital Tools for Management**: Utilizing technology for better communication, project management, and knowledge sharing among family members and stakeholders.

- **Data-Driven Decision Making**: Leveraging analytics for informed decision-making in the succession process.

7. Crisis Preparedness

- **Contingency Planning**: Developing contingency plans to address unexpected events, ensuring business continuity during transitions.

- **Risk Assessment**: Conducting regular risk assessments to identify potential challenges in succession planning.

CHAPTER: 19

Case studies of successful and unsuccessful succession planning in Indian family businesses

Succession planning in Indian family businesses often presents unique challenges and opportunities. Here are examples of both successful and unsuccessful cases:

Successful Succession Planning:

1. TataGroup

- **Overview:** Tata Group, one of India's largest conglomerates, has successfully navigated succession planning through a structured process.

- **Strategy:** The group emphasizes grooming leaders from within, with a focus on meritocracy. Ratan Tata's transition to Cyrus Mistry as chairman was supported by a strong leadership development program.

- **Outcome:** The business-maintained stability and continued growth, demonstrating that strategic planning and transparency can lead to successful transitions.

2. Mahindra & Mahindra

- **Overview:** This automotive and farm equipment giant has effectively planned for succession through a clear governance structure.

- **Strategy:** Anand Mahindra has fostered a culture of innovation and leadership development, ensuring that future leaders are well-prepared.

- **Outcome:** The company has consistently performed well, attributed to its strong leadership pipeline and strategic vision.

Unsuccessful Succession Planning:

1. Kingfisher Airlines

- **Overview:** Founded by Vijay Mallya, Kingfisher Airlines faced severe challenges partly due to poor succession planning.

- **Strategy:** The lack of a robust succession plan led to leadership struggles and operational mismanagement after Mallya's declining influence.

- **Outcome:** The airline eventually shut down, illustrating the consequences of neglecting structured succession planning.

2. Hindustan Motors

- **Overview:** Once a leader in the Indian automobile industry, Hindustan Motors struggled with succession issues.

- **Strategy:** The company failed to prepare the next generation for leadership roles, leading to a lack of vision and strategic direction.

- **Outcome:** The decline in market share and eventual financial troubles highlighted the importance of effective succession planning in maintaining business health.

Key Takeaways:

- **Importance of Governance:** Successful family businesses often implement formal governance structures and succession planning processes.

- **Leadership Development:** Investing in leadership development ensures continuity and resilience.

- **Clear Communication:** Transparent communication about roles and responsibilities is crucial for smooth transitions.

- **Adaptability:** Businesses must adapt to changing market conditions and have flexible plans to navigate unforeseen challenges.

Group: VI

Subject	Chapter No.
Developing a succession plan	20
Steps in creating a succession plan	21
Identifying and grooming potential successors	22
Training and development for successors	23
Structuring ownership and management transitions	24

Leadership and learning are indispensable to each other – John F. Kennedy.

CHAPTER: 20

Developing a Succession Plan -

What is the conducting regular risks assessment to identify potential challenges in succession planning in Indian family-owned businesses?

Conducting regular risk assessments for succession planning involves several key steps to identify potential challenges:

1. Stakeholder Analysis: Identify key family members and non-family stakeholders. Assess their roles, interests, and potential resistance to change.

2. Governance Structures: Evaluate existing governance frameworks. A lack of formal structures can lead to conflicts and unclear roles.

3. Skill Gaps: Assess the competencies of potential successors. Identify any skills or knowledge gaps that could hinder effective leadership.

4. Emotional Dynamics: Analyse family relationships and dynamics. Emotional factors can impact decision-making and succession effectiveness.

5. Financial Stability: Review the financial health of the business. Economic challenges can complicate succession if resources are strained.

6. Market Conditions: Stay informed about industry trends and market conditions that could affect the business's future viability.

7. Legal and Regulatory Compliance: Ensure that all legal aspects of succession planning, such as inheritance laws and business agreements, are up to date.

8. Communication Strategies: Evaluate how succession plans are communicated within the family and organization. Miscommunication can lead to misunderstandings and disputes.

9. Cultural Factors: Consider the impact of cultural values and practices on succession planning. These can influence decision-making and acceptance of successors.

10. Contingency Planning: Develop contingency plans for unexpected events, such as sudden deaths or resignations, to ensure business continuity.

By regularly assessing these areas, family businesses can proactively identify and mitigate risks associated with succession planning.

8. Communication Strategies: Evaluate how succession plans are communicated within the family and organization. Miscommunication can lead to misunderstandings and disputes.

9. Cultural Factors: Consider the impact of cultural values and practices on succession planning. These can influence decision-making and acceptance of successors.

10. Contingency Planning: Develop contingency plans for unexpected events, such as sudden deaths or resignations, to ensure business continuity.

By regularly assessing these areas, family businesses can proactively identify and mitigate risks associated with succession planning.

CHAPTER: 21

Steps in creating a succession plan in family-owned business in India

Creating a succession plan for a family-owned business in India involves several key steps:

1. Assess the Current Situation

• Evaluate the business's strengths, weaknesses, and market position.

• Identify potential successors within the family.

2. Define Goals and Objectives

• Determine what you want to achieve with the succession plan (e.g., continuity, growth, family harmony).

3. Identify Successors

• Evaluate family members for their skills, interests, and commitment.

• Consider external candidates if necessary.

4. Develop a Training Program:

• Create a mentorship system to groom potential successors.

• Provide them with experience in various aspects of the business.

5. Involve Key Stakeholders:

• Engage family members and key employees in discussions about the succession plan.

• Address concerns and ensure alignment on the vision.

6. Document the Plan:

• Write down the succession strategy, including timelines, roles, and responsibilities.

• Include provisions for unexpected events (e.g., sudden illness).

7. Financial Planning:

• Assess the financial implications of the succession, including tax considerations and valuation of the business.

• Plan for any necessary funding or investment.

8. Legal Considerations:

• Consult with legal advisors to address issues related to ownership transfer and estate planning.

• Draft necessary legal documents (wills, trusts, partnership agreements).

9. Communication Strategy:

• Develop a clear communication plan to inform all stakeholders about the succession process.

• Foster an environment of transparency to mitigate conflicts.

10. Monitor and Adjust:

- Regularly review and update the succession plan as circumstances change.

- Ensure that the plan remains relevant and aligned with the business's goals.

11. Implement the Plan:

- Gradually transition responsibilities to the chosen successor.

- Provide ongoing support and feedback during the transition.

CHAPTER: 22

Identifying and grooming potential successors

Identifying and grooming potential successors for a family-owned business in India involves several key criteria:

1. Leadership Skills: Look for candidates who demonstrate strong leadership capabilities, including decision-making, communication, and interpersonal skills.

2. Understanding of Business Operations: Potential successors should have a thorough understanding of the business model, industry dynamics, and operational processes.

3. Cultural Fit: They should align with the family's values and the business's culture to ensure continuity and harmony.

4. Education and Experience: Relevant education, such as business management or finance, along with practical experience in various roles within the business, is essential.

5. Vision and Strategic Thinking: The ability to envision the future of the business and develop strategies for growth is crucial.

6. Adaptability and Innovation: Successors should be open to change and able to implement innovative practices to stay competitive.

7. Emotional Intelligence: Strong emotional intelligence helps in managing relationships, conflict resolution, and fostering a positive work environment.

8. Commitment and Passion: A genuine commitment to the business and a passion for its success are vital for long-term sustainability.

9. Mentorship and Training: Structured mentorship programs can help groom successors, offering them opportunities to learn from experienced leaders within the business.

10. Networking Skills: Building relationships within the industry can enhance the business's profile and opportunities for growth.

11. Succession Planning: Establishing a clear succession plan that includes timelines, roles, and responsibilities can guide the transition effectively. Regular evaluation and adaptation of these criteria can help ensure that the chosen successor is well-prepared to take over the family business.

CHAPTER: 23

Training and development for the successor of a family-owned business in India

Training and development for the successor of a family-owned business in India is crucial for ensuring a smooth transition and long-term success. Here are key strategies to consider:

1. Structured Mentorship

• Pair the successor with experienced family members or senior managers for hands-on learning.

• Encourage regular feedback sessions to discuss challenges and successes.

2. Formal Education

• Consider enrolling the successor in relevant courses or an MBA program focused on business management, finance, or entrepreneurship.

• Attend workshops on leadership and strategic management.

3. Skill Development

• Identify key skills required for the business (e.g., negotiation, financial acumen, marketing).

• Provide opportunities for skill development through workshops or online courses.

4. Exposure to All Departments

- Rotate the successor through various departments (e.g., operations, finance, HR) to gain a holistic understanding of the business.

- Allow involvement in decision-making processes across departments.

5. Networking and Industry Exposure

- Encourage participation in industry conferences and seminars to build a professional network.

- Foster relationships with mentors outside the family business for diverse perspectives.

6. Strategic Planning Involvement

- Include the successor in strategic planning sessions to develop a long-term vision.

- Encourage them to contribute fresh ideas and insights.

7. Cultural and Ethical Training

- Instil the company's values, ethics, and culture through workshops and discussions.

- Highlight the importance of maintaining family legacy while innovating.

8. Conflict Resolution and Governance

- Teach conflict management and resolution strategies, especially in family dynamics.

- Discuss governance structures to ensure transparency and accountability.

9. Continuous Learning and Adaptation

• Promote a culture of continuous improvement and adaptability to market changes.

• Encourage reading and research on industry trends and new technologies.

10. Feedback and Evaluation

• Implement a regular evaluation process to assess progress and areas for improvement.

• Celebrate milestones to build confidence and motivation.

CHAPTER: 24

Structuring ownership and management transition while doing succession planning in family-owned business-

Structuring ownership and management transition in a family-owned business involves careful planning to ensure continuity and preserve family relationships. Here are key steps for effective succession planning:

1. Assessment of Current Situation

• Evaluate the Business: Assess the financial health, market position, and operational strengths.

• Identify Key Roles: Determine which roles are critical for the business's success and how they will transition.

2. Define Succession Objectives

• Family Goals: Clarify what family members want from the business (e.g., legacy, financial returns).

• Business Goals: Align family objectives with long-term business goals.

3. Develop a Succession Plan

• Ownership Structure: Decide on the ownership model (e.g., sole ownership, shared ownership among family members).

• Management Structure: Define who will take over management roles and the timeline for the transition.

4. Identify and Prepare Successors

• Select Potential Leaders: Identify family members or key employees who could fill leadership roles.

• Training and Development: Provide mentorship, training, and experience to prepare successors for their future roles.

5. Create a Communication Plan

• Transparent Discussions: Regularly communicate the succession plan with all stakeholders, including family members and key employees.

• Conflict Resolution: Establish mechanisms to address conflicts that may arise during the transition.

6. Implement Legal and Financial Strategies

• Estate Planning: Work with legal advisors to draft wills, trusts, and other documents that clarify ownership.

• Valuation and Buy-Sell Agreements: Determine the business's value and create agreements for transferring ownership.

7. Monitor and Adjust the Plan

• Regular Reviews: Periodically review the succession plan to adapt to changes in the business or family dynamics.

• Feedback Loop: Encourage feedback from successors and other stakeholders to refine the approach.

8. Cultural and Emotional Considerations

• **Preserving Family Values**: Ensure the transition respects family values and legacy.

• **Emotional Support**: Provide support to family members during the transition, recognizing it can be an emotional process.

Group: VII

Subject	Chapter No.
Governance structures and succession planning	25
Role of family councils and Board of Directors	26
Implementing effective governance structures	27
Balancing family interests with professional management	28

Why do I need succession planning? I'm very alert, I'm very vibrant. I have no intention to retire-**Sheldon Adelson**

CHAPTER: 25

Governance structures and succession planning are crucial for the sustainability and growth in respect to Indian family businesses-
Here's an overview of key aspects:

Governance Structures

1. Family Constitution: Many Indian family businesses create a family constitution that outlines governance principles, roles, responsibilities, and conflict resolution mechanisms. This document helps in managing family dynamics and maintaining focus on business objectives.

2. Board of Directors: Establishing a formal board, often including non-family members, can provide diverse perspectives and professional expertise. This board typically oversees strategy, risk management, and accountability.

3. Advisory Boards: Some families form advisory boards to provide guidance without the formal responsibilities of a board of directors. This can include industry experts who advise on strategic direction.

4. Management Structures: Clear delineation between ownership and management roles is important. Families often hire professional managers to run day-to-day operations, which helps mitigate conflicts between family and business interests.

5. Stakeholder Engagement: Engaging stakeholders, including non-family employees and investors, in decision-making processes fosters transparency and trust, which are vital for long-term success.

Succession Planning

1. **Early Planning**: Successful family businesses often start succession planning early. Identifying potential successors and grooming them over time is critical to ensuring a smooth transition.

2. **Mentoring and Training**: Providing successors with opportunities to gain experience in various business functions is essential. This can include formal education, mentorship from family members, and hands-on experience.

3. **Formal Succession Policies**: Establishing formal policies around succession helps clarify expectations and processes. This can reduce uncertainty and prevent conflicts during transitions.

4. **Communication**: Open discussions about succession among family members can help address fears and expectations. Regular family meetings can facilitate transparency and alignment.

5. **Emotional Preparedness**: Addressing the emotional aspects of succession is crucial. Families need to prepare for potential conflicts and ensure that all members feel valued and heard.

6. **Legal and Financial Planning**: Proper legal and financial frameworks should be established to ensure smooth transitions of ownership. This includes wills, trusts, and tax considerations.

Challenges:

• **Resistance to Change**: Family dynamics can hinder governance reforms and succession planning.

• **Lack of Professionalization**: Many family businesses struggle with balancing family ties and the need for professional management.

• **Conflicts**: Emotional attachments and differing visions for the future can lead to conflicts, making effective governance essential.

CHAPTER: 26

Role of family councils and board of directors in case of succession planning in Indian family-

Succession planning in Indian family-owned businesses is critical for ensuring continuity and stability. Both family councils and boards of directors play vital roles in this process.

Family Councils

1. Facilitating Communication: Family councils promote open dialogue among family members about the future of the business, helping to align interests and values.

2. Defining Roles: They clarify the roles of family members in the business, ensuring that everyone understands their responsibilities and contributions.

3. Conflict Resolution: Family councils provide a structured forum for resolving disputes, which is essential in preserving family harmony during transitions.

4. Strategic Planning: They can help in identifying potential successors and preparing them for leadership roles through mentorship and training.

5. Legacy Preservation: Family councils emphasize the importance of the family's legacy, ensuring that the values and vision that built the business are passed down.

Board of Directors

1. Governance and Oversight: The board provides an objective perspective on succession planning, ensuring that decisions are made in the best interest of the business.

2. Strategic Input: Board members often bring external expertise and experience, helping to formulate a robust succession strategy that aligns with industry trends and best practices.

3. Evaluating Talent: A diverse board can help assess the capabilities of potential successors, ensuring that the chosen individual possesses the necessary skills and vision.

4. Risk Management: The board plays a key role in identifying and mitigating risks associated with succession, including the potential for family conflicts.

5. Ensuring Professionalism: By encouraging professional management practices, the board can help ensure that the business remains competitive and sustainable beyond family leadership.

CHAPTER: 27

Implementing effective governance structures

Balancing family interests with professional management while doing succession planning in Indian family businesses. It involves several key strategies:

1. Establish Clear Governance Structures

• Implement a family constitution that outlines roles, responsibilities, and decision-making processes.

• Create a board that includes both family members and independent directors to ensure diverse perspectives.

2. Define Roles and Responsibilities

• Clearly delineate family and non-family roles to minimize conflicts.

• Establish a professional management team that operates independently while respecting family values.

3. Encourage Open Communication

• Foster a culture of transparency where family members can express their views and concerns.

• Regular family meetings can help address issues and align interests.

4. Develop a Succession Plan Early

• Start succession planning well in advance to identify and groom potential leaders within the family.

• Include training programs for family members to prepare them for leadership roles.

5. Address Emotional Dynamics

• Recognize the emotional aspects of family business dynamics, including legacy concerns and sibling rivalries.

• Facilitate mediation or coaching to navigate these issues effectively.

6. Focus on Professional Development

• Encourage family members to gain external experience and education in their respective fields.

• Consider appointing family members to positions based on merit rather than lineage.

7. Align Interests Through Shared Vision

• Develop a shared vision that integrates family values with business goals, ensuring everyone is aligned.

• Use strategic planning sessions to define long-term objectives.

8. Utilize External Advisors

• Engage consultants or advisors with expertise in family business dynamics to facilitate the planning process.

• External perspectives can help mitigate biases and enhance decision-making.

9. Plan for Financial Succession

• Ensure financial stability by planning for the distribution of assets and the financial health of the business.

• Consider structures like trusts or family investment companies to manage wealth distribution effectively.

10. Monitor and Adapt

• Continuously evaluate the succession plan and make adjustments as needed based on changes in the family or business environment.

• Foster a mindset of adaptability to keep the business resilient.

CHAPTER: 28

Balancing family interests with professional management while doing succession planning in Indian family businesses. It involves several key strategies:

1. Establish Clear Governance Structures

- Implement a family constitution that outlines roles, responsibilities, and decision-making processes.

- Create a board that includes both family members and independent directors to ensure diverse perspectives.

2. Define Roles and Responsibilities

- Clearly delineate family and non-family roles to minimize conflicts.

- Establish a professional management team that operates independently while respecting family values.

3. Encourage Open Communication

- Foster a culture of transparency where family members can express their views and concerns.

- Regular family meetings can help address issues and align interests.

4. Develop a Succession Plan Early

• Start succession planning well in advance to identify and groom potential leaders within the family.

• Include training programs for family members to prepare them for leadership roles.

5. Address Emotional Dynamics

• Recognize the emotional aspects of family business dynamics, including legacy concerns and sibling rivalries.

• Facilitate mediation or coaching to navigate these issues effectively.

6. Focus on Professional Development

• Encourage family members to gain external experience and education in their respective fields.

• Consider appointing family members to positions based on merit rather than lineage.

7. Align Interests Through Shared Vision

• Develop a shared vision that integrates family values with business goals, ensuring everyone is aligned.

• Use strategic planning sessions to define long-term objectives.

8. Utilize External Advisor

Engage consultants or advisors with expertise in family business dynamics to facilitate the planning process.

External perspectives can help mitigate biases and enhance decision-making.

9. Plan for Financial Succession

Ensure financial stability by planning for the distribution of assets and the financial health of the business.

Consider structures like trusts or family investment companies to manage wealth distribution effectively.

10. Monitor and Adapt

Continuously evaluate the succession plan and make adjustments as needed based on changes in the family or business environment.

Foster a mind-set of adaptability to keep the business resilient.

Group: VIII

Subject	Chapter No.
Legal and Financial Considerations for succession planning.	29
Legal Frameworks for succession planning	30
Financial Planning and Asset Management	31
Tax Implications and Estate Planning	32

Responsibility walks hand in hand with capacity and power-Josiah Gilbert Holland.

CHAPTER: 29

Legal and financial consideration in case of succession planning of family-owned businesses in India.

Succession planning in family-owned businesses in India involves several legal and financial considerations:

Legal Considerations

1. Succession Laws:

• Understanding personal laws applicable to family members (Hindu Succession Act, Muslim Personal Law, etc.) is crucial.

• Ensure compliance with the Indian Companies Act for corporate entities.

2. Will and Testament:

• Drafting a clear will to outline the distribution of assets can help avoid disputes.

• Consider registering the will to enhance its legal standing.

3. Partnership Agreements:

• If the business is a partnership, review and amend the partnership deed to reflect succession plans.

4. Property Ownership:

• Clarify ownership of business assets to prevent legal challenges post-succession.

5. Tax Implications:

Be aware of potential inheritance taxes and capital gains taxes upon transfer of ownership.

6. Family Governance Structures:
Establish family councils or governance frameworks to manage conflicts and ensure smooth transitions.

Financial Considerations

1. Valuation of the Business:
Conduct a thorough valuation to determine the fair market value, which is essential for equitable distribution.

2. Funding the Succession:
Plan for liquidity to cover taxes and other expenses that arise during the transfer of assets.

3. Debt Management:
Address any existing debts and ensure that successors understand the financial obligations.

4. Insurance Policies:

Consider life insurance and key person insurance to protect against financial loss during the transition.

5. Investment Strategy:

Develop a long-term investment strategy to maintain and grow business assets after the succession.

6. Financial Education

Provide successors with financial literacy training to ensure they can manage the business effectively.

CHAPTER: 30

Legal framework for succession planning in India e.g. inheritance laws, family settlements

Succession planning in India is governed by various legal frameworks depending on personal laws and the nature of the property involved. Here are the key aspects:

1. Personal Laws

• Hindu Succession Act, 1956: Governs inheritance for Hindus, covering both intestate (without a will) and testate (with a will) succession. It emphasizes equal rights for sons and daughters in ancestral property.

• Muslim Personal Law (Shariat) Application Act, 1937: Governs succession for Muslims, with specific rules on inheritance shares for heirs, usually favouring male heirs.

• Indian Succession Act, 1925: Applies to Christians, Parsis, and others, providing a comprehensive framework for wills and intestate succession.

2. Wills and Testaments

• Individuals can create wills to specify the distribution of their property upon death. The Act requires certain formalities, such as attestation by witnesses.

3. Family Settlements

• Informal agreements among family members can facilitate the division of property and avoid disputes. While these are generally not legally binding, they can be documented and sometimes registered to give them greater legal standing.

4. Registration of Property

• Property transfer should be properly documented and registered to ensure clarity in ownership and succession.

5. Gift Deeds

• Property can be transferred during a person's lifetime through gift deeds, which can help in succession planning and avoiding future disputes.

6. Trusts

• Establishing trusts can be an effective succession planning tool, allowing for controlled distribution of assets and minimizing tax implications.

7. Legal Framework for Disputes

• The Civil Procedure Code and specific family courts handle disputes arising from succession matters, including claims for maintenance and inheritance.

8. Tax Implications

• Succession can have tax implications, including estate duty (though currently abolished) and income tax on inherited assets.
Proper planning can mitigate tax burdens

CHAPTER: 31

Financial Planning & Asset Management Financial planning and assets management in the succession planning in India in case of family businesses. Succession planning in family businesses in India is critical for ensuring continuity and stability. Here's an overview of financial planning and asset management aspects:

1. Assessment of Current Assets

• Valuation: Regularly assess the value of all business assets, including real estate, equipment, and intellectual property.

• Inventory Management: Maintain an accurate inventory to ensure all assets are accounted for.

2. Legal Framework

• Wills and Trusts: Establish clear legal documents to outline asset distribution. Trusts can help manage tax liabilities and protect assets.

• Compliance: Ensure compliance with Indian laws, including the Hindu Succession Act, which governs inheritance for Hindu families.

3. Financial Planning

• Cash Flow Analysis: Regularly analyse cash flow to ensure the business can support family needs during the transition.

• Debt Management: Evaluate existing debts and plan for their management to prevent financial strain during succession.

4. Investment Strategy

• Diversification: Create a diversified investment portfolio to protect against market volatility.

• Reinvestment: Consider reinvesting profits into the business to support growth and stability during the transition.

5. Education and Involvement of Successors

• Training: Provide financial and managerial training to the next generation.

• Mentorship: Encourage involvement in decision-making processes to prepare successors for leadership roles.

6. Family Governance Structures

• Family Council: Establish a family council to discuss and manage family-related business decisions and conflicts.

• Clear Roles: Define roles and responsibilities to minimize conflicts and ensure clarity in operations.

7. Tax Planning

• Minimize Liabilities: Engage tax professionals to explore options for minimizing tax liabilities during and after the succession process.

• Gifting Strategies: Consider gifting assets during the founders' lifetime to reduce the taxable estate.

8. Contingency Planning

• Crisis Management: Prepare for unexpected events (e.g., death or incapacity of key members) to ensure business continuity.

• Insurance: Utilize life insurance and key person insurance to mitigate financial risks.

CHAPTER: 32

Tax Implications and Estate Planning

Tax implications and estate planning in succession planning of Indian Succession planning in Indian family businesses involves careful consideration of both tax implications and estate planning. Here are key points to consider:

Tax Implications

1. **Income Tax**: Transfers of business assets can attract capital gains tax. Proper valuation and timing of asset transfers can mitigate tax liabilities.

2. **Wealth Tax:** Though abolished, previous wealth tax implications on the valuation of family businesses should be considered if any liabilities exist from earlier assessments.

3. **Gift Tax**: Transfers of shares or assets to family members may attract gift tax, especially if the valuation exceeds the threshold limits.

4. **Corporate Tax:** If the business is structured as a corporation, changing ownership can have corporate tax implications, particularly concerning retained earnings and accumulated profits.

5. **Indirect Taxes:** Goods and Services Tax (GST) may apply on the transfer of goods and services during succession.

Estate Planning

1. **Wills and Trusts:** Establishing a clear will or trust is crucial. This helps in the smooth transfer of assets and minimizes disputes.

2. **Family Agreements**: Creating a family constitution or agreement can outline roles, responsibilities, and succession plans, reducing conflicts.

3. **Business Structure**: Choosing the right structure (proprietorship, partnership, LLP, or corporation) can affect succession and tax obligations. For example, LLPs offer limited liability and ease of transfer.

4. **Dispute Resolution Mechanisms**: Including clauses for mediation or arbitration can help resolve family disputes amicably.

5. **Compliance and Documentation:** Keeping accurate records and ensuring compliance with regulatory requirements can prevent legal issues during succession.

Best Practices

- **Professional Advisory:** Engaging with legal, tax, and financial advisors ensures that the plan is comprehensive and compliant with laws.

- **Regular Review:** Periodically reviewing the succession plan helps accommodate changes in family dynamics or business structure.

- **Communication**: Open discussions among family members about succession plans can reduce misunderstandings and foster unity.

Group: IX

Subject	Chapter No.
Detailed analysis of successful succession planning in Indian Family businesses (e.g. Infosys, Mahindra Group)	33
Examination of Challenges faced and lessons learned from unsuccessful succession cases (e.g. Kingfisher Airlines, Ranbaxy)	34

Life is a succession of lessons which must be lived to be understood. All is riddle, and the key to a riddle is another riddle- Ralph Waldo Emerson

CHAPTER: 33

Detailed analysis of successful succession planning in Indian family businesses (e.g., Infosys, Mahindra Group)

Succession planning in Indian family businesses is a critical process that ensures continuity and long-term sustainability. Notable examples include Infosys and the Mahindra Group, both of which have navigated succession challenges successfully. Here's a detailed analysis of their approaches:

1. Infosys: Strategic Transition

Founders' Vision and Governance: Infosys, co-founded by N.R. Narayana Murthy and his peers, established a clear governance framework. The transition from a founder-led to a professional management model was strategic, involving the appointment of capable CEOs like Nandan Nilekani and later Vishal Sikka. Professionalization: Infosys embraced a professional management culture early on. The board included independent directors, which fostered accountability and diverse perspectives in decision-making.

Leadership Development: The company invested heavily in leadership development programs, identifying and nurturing talent within the organization. This pipeline ensured that successors were groomed for leadership roles, facilitating a smoother transition.

Crisis Management: Infosys faced challenges during transitions, particularly with public scrutiny around leadership changes. By maintaining transparency and involving stakeholders in the process, the company mitigated potential backlash.

2. Mahindra Group: Diverse Leadership and Resilience

Cultural Foundations: The Mahindra Group, founded in 1945, has emphasized a strong cultural ethos that values innovation and adaptability. This culture is integral to its succession planning, fostering an environment where successors can thrive.

Decentralized Structure: Mahindra operates with a decentralized structure that allows individual business units to thrive independently. This autonomy encourages entrepreneurial leadership, making it easier to identify and promote successors within each unit.

Strategic External Appointments: The group has occasionally brought in external talent to lead key divisions, enhancing diversity in thought and leadership styles. This approach helps blend traditional family business values with contemporary corporate practices.

Focus on Legacy and Vision: Mahindra's succession strategy emphasizes the importance of legacy. Leaders are chosen not only for their operational capabilities but also for their alignment with the group's broader vision, particularly in areas like sustainability and social responsibility.

3. Key Elements of Successful Succession Planning

a. Early Preparation:

Both companies demonstrate the importance of early and deliberate preparation for succession. This involves identifying potential leaders and providing them with diverse experiences.

b. Leadership Development Programs:

Ongoing training and mentorship are crucial. Companies like Infosys have robust programs to cultivate leadership skills among younger employees, ensuring a ready pool of candidates.

c. Transparent Communication:

Successful transitions involve open lines of communication with stakeholders, including family members, employees, and shareholders. Transparency helps build trust and reduces uncertainties.

d. Embracing Change:

Adapting to change is vital. Both Infosys and Mahindra have shown flexibility in their succession strategies, evolving their approaches based on market dynamics and organizational needs.

e. Legacy Planning:

Understanding and planning for the legacy of the founder or previous leaders is essential. Both firms have integrated their founders' values into their succession plans, ensuring continuity of vision.

4. Challenges and Mitigation Strategies

a. Family Dynamics:

Family conflicts can complicate succession. Proactive mediation and clear governance structures can help mitigate these issues, as seen in Mahindra's practices.

b. Resistance to Change:

Some stakeholders may resist new leadership styles. Both companies address this by emphasizing the importance of innovation while respecting traditional values.

c. Market Volatility:

Market changes can impact succession decisions. Agility in leadership selection and the ability to adapt quickly to external conditions are crucial, as demonstrated by Infosys during its transitions.

CHAPTER: 34

Examination of challenges faced and lessons learned from unsuccessful succession cases (e.g. Kingfisher Airlines, Ranbaxy) in Indian family businesses

Examining the challenges and lessons learned from unsuccessful succession cases in Indian family businesses, such as Kingfisher Airlines and Ranbaxy, reveals critical insights.

Challenges Faced:

1. Lack of Clear Succession Planning: Many family businesses, including Kingfisher Airlines, lacked a structured plan for transitioning leadership. This led to confusion and conflict over who should take charge.

2. Family Conflicts: Personal rivalries and power struggles often overshadowed business interests. In Ranbaxy, disputes among family members affected decision-making and strategic direction.

3. Inadequate Governance Structures: Weak corporate governance can hinder effective decision-making. Both companies suffered from a lack of formal mechanisms to manage leadership transitions and accountability.

4. Loss of Vision and Strategy: Unsuccessful succession often leads to a drift in strategic vision. Kingfisher Airlines expanded aggressively without a sustainable business model, ultimately leading to its downfall.

5. Financial Mismanagement: Poor financial oversight during transitions can exacerbate challenges. Ranbaxy faced regulatory issues and financial strain, impacting its reputation and operations.

Lessons Learned

1. Importance of Formal Succession Planning: Establishing a clear and documented succession plan is essential. This should include training and mentoring the next generation well in advance.

2. Strengthening Governance: Implementing robust governance structures, such as advisory boards or family councils, can help mitigate conflicts and align family and business goals.

3. Focus on Professional Management: Engaging non-family professionals can bring objectivity and expertise, essential for navigating complex business landscapes and ensuring operational efficiency.

4. Cultivating a Unified Vision: A shared vision among family members can drive cohesion. Regular discussions and strategic planning sessions can help align interests and goals.

5. Financial Prudence: Ensuring sound financial practices and regular audits can prevent mismanagement. Transparency in financial dealings is crucial for maintaining trust.

6. Adaptability and Learning: Family businesses must be willing to adapt to changing market dynamics and learn from past mistakes. Embracing innovation and flexibility can enhance resilience.

Group: X

The Role External Advisors

Subject	Chapter No.
Importance of involving external advisors (e.g. Consultants, legal experts, financial advisors)	35
How to select and work with external advisors	36
Case studies of successful interventions by external advisors	37

"To be successful, succession planning teams must identify the core competencies required for a broad range of key positions, including those that may not even exist today." – Todd Hoffman and Stanley Womack

CHAPTER: 35

Importance of involving external advisors (e.g. consultants, legal expert, financial advisors,) in the succession planning of Indian family businesses. Involving external advisors in the succession planning of Indian family businesses is crucial for several reasons

1. Objective Perspective: External advisors provide an unbiased viewpoint, helping to identify potential issues that family members may overlook due to emotional ties.

2. Expertise and Experience: Consultants, legal experts, and financial advisors bring specialized knowledge and experience in governance, tax implications, and regulatory compliance, which are essential for effective succession planning.

3. Structured Process: They help in creating a structured succession plan, ensuring all aspects are covered, from leadership roles to estate management, which can be complex in family-owned businesses.

4. Conflict Resolution: External advisors can facilitate discussions and mediate conflicts among family members, helping to maintain harmony and focus on business objectives.

5. Future-proofing the Business: Their insights can help identify market trends and strategic opportunities, ensuring the business remains competitive post-succession.

6. Legal Compliance: Legal experts ensure that the succession plan complies with Indian laws, helping to avoid future disputes and legal challenges.

7. Financial Planning: Financial advisors assist in structuring the financial aspects of the transition, ensuring the business's sustainability and growth during and after the succession process.

CHAPTER: 36

How to select and work with External Advisor in case, of the Succession Planning in family businesses.

Selecting and working with external advisors for succession planning in family businesses in India involves several key steps:

1. Identify Your Needs

• Assess Goals: Determine what you want to achieve with succession planning (e.g., leadership transition, wealth distribution).

• Define Areas of Expertise: Identify specific areas where you need guidance, such as legal, financial, or operational aspects.

2. Research Potential Advisors

• Experience with Family Businesses: Look for advisors with a proven track record in family business succession planning.

• Cultural Compatibility: Ensure they understand the cultural dynamics of family businesses in India.

3. Evaluate Qualifications

• Certifications and Credentials: Check their qualifications and relevant certifications.

• Client Testimonials: Seek feedback from other family businesses that have worked with them.

4. Conduct Interviews

• Discuss Experience: Ask about their previous work with similar businesses.

• Assess Approach: Evaluate their methodology and how they plan to involve family members in the process.

5. Establish Clear Roles

• Define Responsibilities: Clearly outline the roles of advisors versus family members in the succession process.

• Set Expectations: Discuss timelines, deliverables, and communication protocols.

6. Foster Open Communication

• Regular Updates: Schedule regular check-ins to discuss progress and address concerns.

• Encourage Feedback: Create an environment where family members feel comfortable sharing their thoughts.

7. Monitor and Adjust

• Review Progress: Periodically assess the effectiveness of the advisors and the succession plan.

• Be Flexible: Be open to adjusting the plan based on feedback and changing circumstances.

8. Ensure Legal Compliance

• Legal Advisors: Engage legal experts to navigate regulatory requirements and ensure the plan is compliant with Indian laws.

9. Plan for Implementation

• Transition Strategy: Work with advisors to create a comprehensive strategy for transitioning leadership.

• Training and Development: Invest in training the next generation to prepare them for leadership roles.

CHAPTER: 37

Case studies of successful intervention by external advisors in case of succession planning in Indian family businesses-

Here are a few case studies that illustrate successful interventions by external advisors in succession planning within Indian family businesses:

1. Tata Group

Background: Tata Group, one of India's largest conglomerates, faced succession challenges as founder Jamshedji Tata's health declined.

Intervention: The group brought in external advisors to assess potential successors and facilitate leadership training. They conducted workshops focusing on governance structures and strategic decision-making.

Outcome: The transition to Ratan Tata was smooth, with clearly defined roles and responsibilities, helping the group maintain stability and continue its growth trajectory.

2. Wipro Limited

Background: Wipro's founder, Azim Premji, needed to prepare for a leadership transition amid changing market dynamics.

Intervention: Wipro engaged external consultants to develop a formal succession plan that included leadership training programs and an assessment of internal talent. Outcome: The company successfully transitioned to a new leadership team, maintaining its competitive edge and continuing to innovate, demonstrating the importance of structured planning.

3. Mahindra Group

Background: With diverse interests and multiple family members involved, Mahindra Group faced complexity in succession planning.

Intervention: External advisors were brought in to facilitate family meetings, clarify roles, and establish governance frameworks.

Outcome: This led to the creation of a Family Constitution, which outlined the vision and values of the group, ensuring a coherent approach to succession and decision-making.

4. Godrej Group

Background: Godrej needed to manage succession while expanding its business portfolio and navigating market challenges.

Intervention: External advisors helped establish a structured governance model and succession plan, which included identifying and grooming future leaders within the family and organization.

Outcome: The transition to the next generation was well-managed, allowing Godrej to adapt and thrive in various sectors, demonstrating the effectiveness of strategic planning.

5. Birla Group

Background: The Birla Group, with its extensive lineage, faced potential fragmentation and leadership challenges.

Intervention: The family engaged external advisors to facilitate discussions on succession planning, fostering unity among family members and aligning their interests.

Outcome: The group successfully navigated leadership transitions, ensuring continued collaboration and growth across its diverse business segments.

Key Takeaways

• *Importance of External Advisors: They provide objective perspectives, facilitate family discussions, and help establish governance frameworks.*

• *Structured Planning: A formal succession plan can mitigate risks and ensure a smooth transition.*

• *Training and Development: Investing in leadership training for potential successors is crucial for long-term success.*

• *Family Governance: Establishing clear roles and responsibilities within the family helps maintain unity and direction.*

Group: XI

Future Trends in Succession Planning.

Subject	Chapter No.
Emerging Trends in succession planning globally and in India	38
Impact of Technology and Globalization on family-owned businesses	39
Preparing for Future challenges and Opportunities	40

No burden is so heavy for a man to bear as a succession of happy days-Max Planck

CHAPTER: 38

Emerging trends in succession planning globally and in India
Emerging trends in succession planning globally and in India include

Global Trends:

1. **Diversity and Inclusion**: Organizations are prioritizing diverse leadership pipelines to reflect broader demographics and improve decision-making.

2. **Technology Integration**: Tools like AI and analytics are being used to identify potential leaders and assess their readiness, improving the efficiency of succession planning.

3. **Continuous Development**: Succession planning is evolving from a one-time event to a continuous process, with ongoing leadership development programs.

4. **Remote Leadership Skills**: The rise of remote work has necessitated the development of skills related to managing virtual teams effectively.

5. **Employee Engagement**: Engaging employees in the succession process fosters a culture of transparency and encourages retention.

Trends in India:

1. **Family Business Dynamics**: With a significant portion of businesses being family-owned, there's a growing focus on preparing the next generation for leadership roles.

2. **Skill Development Initiatives**: Companies are increasingly investing in upskilling and reskilling their workforce to ensure a pipeline of capable leaders.

3. **Adoption of Global Best Practices:** Indian companies are beginning to adopt international succession planning frameworks, balancing local cultural nuances.

4. **Focus on Soft Skills:** Emphasizing emotional intelligence, adaptability, and communication skills as critical components for future leaders.

5. **Regulatory Influence:** Government policies are beginning to influence corporate governance practices, impacting how succession planning is approached. These trends highlight the evolving nature of succession planning, driven by both global influences and local contexts.

CHAPTER: 39

Impact of technology and globalisation on family-owned businesses in respect to India

The impact of technology and globalization on family-owned businesses in India is significant and multifaceted:

Technology

1. Operational Efficiency: Adoption of digital tools and software has streamlined operations, reduced costs and enhancing productivity.

2. Market Reach: E-commerce platforms enable family businesses to access broader markets, including international customers, which can significantly increase sales.

3. Data Utilization: Technology allows for better data collection and analysis, helping businesses understand consumer behaviour and tailor their offerings accordingly.

4. Innovation: Increased access to information fosters innovation in product development and service delivery, allowing family businesses to remain competitive.

5. Remote Work: Technology facilitates remote working, which can help family businesses adapt to changing workforce dynamics.

Globalization

1. Increased Competition: Globalization exposes family-owned businesses to international competitors, necessitating higher standards in quality and service.

2. Supply Chain Diversification: Access to global supply chains can reduce costs and improve resource availability, but it also requires businesses to manage complexities.

3. Cultural Exchange: Exposure to global markets introduces diverse consumer preferences, prompting family businesses to adapt their products and marketing strategies.

4. Investment Opportunities: Globalization opens avenues for foreign investment, which can provide necessary capital for expansion.

5. Regulatory Challenges: Operating in a global environment often involves navigating complex regulations, which can be challenging for family-run enterprises.

CHAPTER: 40

Preparing for future challenges and opportunities in respect to succession planning in Indian family businesses

Succession planning in Indian family businesses is crucial for ensuring continuity and sustainable growth. Here are key aspects to consider for preparing for future challenges and opportunities:

1. Understanding Family Dynamics

• **Open Communication**: Foster a culture of transparency within the family to address expectations, aspirations, and concerns.

• **Conflict Resolution**: Establish mechanisms for resolving disputes to maintain harmony and focus on the business.

2. Defining Roles and Responsibilities

• **Clear Hierarchies**: Clearly define roles within the business to prevent overlaps and confusion.

• **Professionalization**: Consider introducing non-family professionals to bring expertise and impartiality.

3. Talent Development

• **Training Programs**: Invest in leadership development and training for the next generation to prepare them for management roles.

• **Mentorship**: Pair younger family members with experienced leaders for guidance and knowledge transfer.

4. Strategic Planning

• **Long-term Vision**: Develop a clear vision for the business that aligns with family values and market opportunities.

• **Adaptability**: Stay responsive to market changes, technology advancements, and emerging business models.

5. Governance Structures

• **Family Councils**: Establish family governance bodies to discuss strategic decisions and family matters.

• **Advisory Boards:** Create boards with external members to provide objective insights and advice.

6. Legal and Financial Considerations

• **Estate Planning:** Ensure that legal frameworks are in place for asset distribution to avoid future conflicts.

• **Financial Literacy**: Equip family members with financial knowledge to make informed decisions about the business.

7. Cultural Sensitivity

• **Respecting Traditions:** Balance modern business practices with traditional values that influence family decisions.

• **Diversity and Inclusion**: Embrace diverse perspectives within the family and the business.

8. Succession Models

- **Identify Successors Early:** Start grooming potential successors well in advance of actual transitions.

- **Exit Strategies**: Develop clear plans for potential exits of current leaders to ensure smooth transitions.

9. Monitoring and Evaluation

- **Regular Reviews**: Implement periodic assessments of succession plans and business performance.

- **Adaptation:** Be willing to adapt the succession strategy as circumstances change

Group: XII
Conclusion

Subject	Chapter No.
Summary of Key Points	41
Final thoughts on the importance of effective succession planning	42
Recommendations for family-owned businesses in India	43

Man approaches the unattainable truth through a succession of errors-Aldous Huxley

CHAPTER: 41

Summary of key points in case of succession planning in Indian family businesses. Succession planning in Indian family businesses involves several key points

1. Early Planning: Start planning for succession early to ensure a smooth transition and avoid conflicts.

2. Clear Structure: Establish a formal governance structure, including roles and responsibilities for family members and non-family executives.

3. Communication: Maintain open communication among family members to address expectations, aspirations, and potential conflicts.

4. Skill Development: Invest in training and development for the next generation to prepare them for leadership roles.

5. Formalization of Processes: Document processes and policies regarding succession to create transparency and reduce ambiguity.

6. Conflict Resolution Mechanisms: Establish mechanisms for resolving disputes to ensure family harmony and business continuity.

7. Legal and Financial Planning: Involve legal and financial advisors to address tax implications, estate planning, and compliance issues.

8. Family Constitution: Develop a family constitution that outlines values, vision, and governance practices to guide decision-making.

9. Engagement of External Advisors: Consider involving external consultants for unbiased perspectives on succession planning.

10. Focus on Legacy: Emphasize the family's legacy and values to maintain cohesion and direction throughout the transition process.

CHAPTER: 42

Final thoughts on the importance of effective succession planning in Indian family businesses

Effective succession planning is crucial for Indian family businesses for several reasons:

1. Sustainability: It ensures continuity and stability, helping the business navigate leadership transitions smoothly and maintain its competitive edge.

2. Conflict Resolution: Proper planning mitigates potential family conflicts and disputes over leadership roles and ownership, fostering harmony within the family.

3. Talent Development: Identifying and nurturing potential successors prepares the next generation, ensuring they possess the necessary skills and vision to lead.

4. Legacy Preservation: Succession planning helps preserve the family's legacy and values, aligning the future direction of the business with its historical roots.

5. Adaptability: It encourages a forward-thinking approach, allowing businesses to adapt to changing market dynamics and innovations, crucial for long-term success.

Overall, effective succession planning is vital for the longevity and resilience of family businesses in India, safeguarding their heritage while preparing for future challenges. Effective succession planning in family-owned businesses is crucial for ensuring long-term stability and success. It helps preserve family legacy, maintain continuity in leadership, and mitigate potential conflicts. By proactively addressing issues related to ownership transfer, skill gaps, and leadership roles, families can safeguard their business against disruption. Additionally, clear succession plans foster a culture of transparency and accountability, which can enhance employee morale and customer confidence. Ultimately, thoughtful planning not only protects the business's future but also strengthens family relationships and values.

CHAPTER: 43

Recommendation for succession planning in family-owned businesses in India

Succession planning in family-owned businesses in India is crucial for ensuring longevity and stability. Here are some recommendations:

1. Early Planning: Begin the succession planning process early to allow for a smooth transition. Identify potential successors and involve them in decision-making.

2. Formal Governance Structure: Establish a formal governance framework that includes a board of directors or advisory board to provide guidance and oversight.

3. Clear Communication: Maintain open communication among family members about roles, expectations, and business strategies to avoid conflicts.

4. Skills Development: Invest in training and development for potential successors to ensure they acquire the necessary skills and experience.

5. Written Succession Plan: Create a documented succession plan outlining the roles, responsibilities, and timelines for the transition.

6. Professional Advice: Seek input from external advisors, such as lawyers, accountants, and consultants, to address legal, financial, and operational issues.

7. Conflict Resolution Mechanism: Establish clear mechanisms for conflict resolution to address disputes amicably and maintain family harmony.

8. Exit Strategies for Current Leaders: Define exit strategies for current leaders, ensuring they remain involved in a supportive capacity as needed.

9. Legacy and Values: Emphasize the importance of the family's values and legacy in the business, ensuring they are passed down to the next generation.

10. Periodic Review: Regularly review and update the succession plan to adapt to changing circumstances and business environments.

Implementing these strategies can help family-owned businesses in India navigate the complexities of succession and secure their future.

Group: XIII

Appendices:

Subject	Chapter No.
Sample of succession Planning Templates	44
List of Useful resources and readings	45
Glossary of Terms	46

I think we're ready for succession. We just must try to do it right- Ellen Johnson Sirleaf

CHAPTER: 44

Sample succession planning templates for family-owned businesses

Here are some sample templates for succession planning in family-owned businesses in India:

1. Succession Planning Framework

Objective:

- Define the purpose and goals of succession planning.

Business Overview:

- Brief description of the business, including history, vision, and mission.

Key Roles:

- List of key positions within the organization.

Succession Candidates:

- Identify potential successors for each key role, including qualifications and experience.

2. Succession Planning Timeline

Activity Responsible Party Deadline Status

Identify key roles Management [Date] [Not Started/In Progress/Completed]

Evaluate potential successors Board/Management [Date] [Not Started/In Progress/Completed]

Develop training plans HR/Management [Date] [Not Started/In Progress/Completed]

Review and finalize plans Family Council [Date] [Not Started/In Progress/Completed]

3. Successor Development Plan

Successor Name Current Position Desired Position Development Needs Timeline [Name] [Position] [Position] [Training/Experience Needed] [Timeline]

4. Family Governance Structure

Family Council:

- Define the roles and responsibilities of family members.

Decision-Making Process:

- Outline how decisions will be made regarding business direction and succession.

Conflict Resolution Mechanism:

- Establish processes for addressing disputes within the family.

5. Exit Strategy for Current Leaders Current Leader(s):

- Name and role of current leader.

Retirement Plan:

• Timeline and conditions for retirement.

Knowledge Transfer:

• Strategies for transferring knowledge and responsibilities.

6. Communication Plan

Stakeholders:
• Identify internal and external stakeholders involved in succession planning.
Communication Strategies:

• Outline how and when communication will occur regarding succession planning.

7. Legal Considerations

Ownership Structure:

• Description of the current ownership and any proposed changes.
Estate Planning:

• Overview of estate planning measures for family members.
Legal Documentation:

• List of documents needed (e.g., wills, trusts, shareholder agreements).

Implementation Tips

1. Engage Family Members: Involve all relevant family members early in the planning process.

2. Regular Review: Schedule regular reviews of the succession plan to adapt to changing circumstances.

3. Professional Guidance: Consider hiring consultants or legal advisors to assist with the process.

CHAPTER: 45

List of Useful Resources & Readings:

List of useful resources & readings in respect of succession planning in family owned businesses in India

Here's a list of useful resources and readings on succession planning in family-owned businesses in India:

Books

1. "Family Business Succession: Your Roadmap to Continuity" by John L. Ward
2. "The Family Business: Its Governance for Sustainability" by K. S. Shyam Sundar
3. "Family Business: Key Issues" by R. Carlock and J. Ward

Articles and Journals

1. "Succession Planning in Indian Family Businesses" - Indian Journal of Family Business
2. "The Role of Trust in Succession Planning" - Family Business Review
3. "Governance in Family Firms: A Study of Indian Business Families" - Journal of Family Business Strategy

Reports and Case Studies

1. EY Family Business Report - Provides insights and trends in family businesses globally, including India.
2. KPMG Family Business Survey - Focuses on challenges and strategies of family-owned enterprises.

3. "Navigating the Succession Landscape in Indian Family Businesses" - A detailed report by Deloitte.

Online Resources

1. Family Business Network (FBN) - Offers various resources and networking opportunities.
2. Institute for Family Business (IFB) - Provides guidance on governance and succession issues.
3. NITI Aayog Publications - Contains studies and recommendations regarding family-owned enterprises.

Workshops and Webinars

1. Family Business Workshops - Various organizations offer specialized workshops focusing on succession planning.
2. Webinars by FBN India - Cover various topics relevant to family business governance and succession.

Consulting Firms

1. Bain & Company - Provides insights on strategic planning and succession in family businesses.
2. McKinsey & Company - Offers resources and case studies on managing family business transitions.

These resources can provide comprehensive insights and practical guidance on succession planning specific to the Indian context.

CHAPTER: 46

Glossary of terms in respect to succession planning in family-owned businesses:

Here's a glossary of key terms related to succession planning in family-owned businesses in India:

Glossary of Terms

1. **Succession Planning:** The process of identifying and developing new leaders to replace old leaders when they leave or retire.

2. **Family Business:** A business owned and operated by members of a family, often spanning multiple generations.

3. **Governance:** The framework of rules and practices by which a family business is directed and controlled, often involving a family constitution or advisory board.

4. **Family Constitution:** A document that outlines the family's values, vision, mission, and rules for managing the family business, including succession planning.

5. **Heir:** An individual, typically a family member, designated to inherit ownership and leadership of the business.

6. **Leadership Development:** The process of preparing family members to take on leadership roles through training, mentorship, and hands-on experience.

7. **Stakeholders:** Individuals or groups with an interest in the business, including family members, employees, customers, suppliers, and investors.

8. Transition Period: The timeframe during which leadership changes from one generation to the next, often requiring careful planning and management.

9. Business Valuation: The process of determining the economic value of a family business, crucial for succession planning and potential buyouts.

10. Family Dynamics: The relationships and interactions among family members, which can significantly impact decision-making in succession planning.

11. Exit Strategy: A plan for how current leaders will leave the business and how ownership will be transferred, ensuring a smooth transition.

12. Mentorship: A relationship in which a more experienced family member guides a younger member in developing their skills and understanding of the business.

13. Professionalization: The process of establishing formal management practices and structures in a family business, often necessary for smooth succession.

14. Conflict Resolution: Strategies and processes for addressing disputes among family members that may arise during succession planning.

Group: XIV

Subject	Chapter No.
Comprehensive list of sources and references used throughout the Book	47

CHAPTER: 47

Comprehensive list of sources and references used for writing this book on succession planning in family-owned businesses in Indian context with examples

For writing a comprehensive book on succession planning in family-owned businesses in the Indian context, you should consider a wide range of sources and references to ensure depth and accuracy. Here's a structured list to guide your research:

1. Books

- *General Succession Planning and Family Business*

- *"Family Business Succession: Your Roadmap to Continuity" by Mark L. Green*

- *"Succession Planning for Family Businesses: A Practical Guide" by Greg McCann and Dan Schneider*
- *"The Family Business: Its Governance for Sustainability" by Alfredo De Massis, Joe Astrachan, and Kelin E. Gersick*
- *IndianContext*

- *"Family Business in India: An Evolutionary Perspective" by K. L. Bhatia*

- *"The Dynamics of Family Business in India" by Sangeeta Singh*

- *"The India Way: How India's Top Business Leaders Are Revolutionizing Management" by Peter Cappelli and Harbir Singh*

2. Academic Journals and Articles

- *International Journals*

- *Journal of Family Business Strategy*

- *Family Business Review*

- *Journal of Family Business Management*

- *Indian Journals*

- *Indian Journal of Corporate Governance*

- *IIMB Management Review*

3. Case Studies and Reports

- *Indian Family Business Case Studies*

- *Harvard Business School Case Studies on Indian family businesses*

- *IIM Ahmedabad and IIM Bangalore case studies*

- *Industry Reports*

- *PwC's Family Business Survey*

- *Deloitte's Global Family Business Survey*

- *EY's Family Business Center Reports*

4. Legal and Regulatory Framework

• Indian Laws and Regulations

• Companies Act, 2013 (India)

• Indian Trusts Act, 1882

• Income Tax Act, 1961

• Legal Commentary and Guides

• Legal commentaries on family business governance and succession

5. Interviews and Biographies

• Biographies of Prominent Indian Business Families

• "The Marwaris: From Jagat Seth to the Birla's" by Ruth Harris

• "Business Maharajas" by Gita Piramal

• Interviews with Family Business Leaders

• Interviews published in business magazines like Business Today, Forbes India, and Economic Times

6. Government and Institutional Publications

• Government Reports and White Papers

- Ministry of Corporate Affairs, Government of India reports

- Institutional Publications

- Reports from institutions like National Institute for Transforming India (NITI Aayog)

7. Industry Associations and Networks

- Family Business Networks

- Confederation of Indian Industry (CII) Family Business Network

- Indian Chamber of Commerce (ICC) publications and events

8. Online Resources and Databases

- Family Business Websites

- Family Business Institute (FBI)

- Family Business Alliance

- Business News Websites

- Business Standard, Mint, and Economic Times archives

- Academic Databases

- JSTOR, Google Scholar, and Research Gate

9. Consultancy and Advisory Firms

• Consulting Firms Specializing in Family Businesses

• Reports and white papers from firms like McKinsey & Company, BCG, and KPMG

10. Workshops and Conferences

• Family Business Conferences

• Materials from conferences held by family business organizations and academic institutions.

Acknowledgement

I acknowledge all the writers of the books and contributors of various research papers and articles taken from academic journals, case studies, reports, legal reports and reports of various interviews, biographies, Government and Institutional Publications, |Industry Associations and Networks, Online Research Resources and data bases, various proceedings of workshops and conferences as I mentioned in the Chapter 47 of this books.

I did my research on the subject of Succession Planning in selecting a Leader of Family-owned businesses in Indian context from various sources on the internet.

My Son Dr Shashanka Dhanuka and daughter-in-law Jyoti Dhanuka who encouraged and helped me in writing this book.

My friend Mr. A.C. Dadhich inspired me to write this book.

My Secretary Mr. Sandip Kumar Das who helped in preparing the manuscript.

www.ingramcontent.com/pod-product-compliance
Lightning Source LLC
Chambersburg PA
CBHW082249220526
45469CB00009B/2937